A Path to Healing:

Journeying Forward After a Loss

To Kathy
life is precious
Barbara Rand Ryan

Barbara Rand Ryan

"Do not go gentle into that good night. Rage…rage…
against the dying of the light."

-Dylan Thomas

DEDICATION

For my husband, Dennis M. Ryan
You were one of a kind and for a moment you were all mine.

A Path to Healing

Contents

Acknowledgements   vi
Forward - Trevor Hough   xii
Author's Note   xiv

Poems
Eleven Weeks   1
Too Late?   2
Final Moment   3
You   4
Nighttime   5
No Final Good-bye   6
Is Death a Better Place for You?   7
Life or Death   8
Dreams   9
When   10
Torch   11
My Hero Soldier   12
Blown Away   13
Cry   14
Remember   15
Alone   16
Relief   17
Tired   18
The Beast   19
Wishing   20
Painful Place   21
Time   22
Fate   23
Who   24
Bad Dream   25
One More Time   26
Do You Still Sparkle?   27
Six Weeks   28
Dark   29

Fourth of July	30
The Truth About Life	31
Come Back	32
Are You Okay?	33
July Third	34
Goodbye	35
Widow	36
If Only	37
As I Get Ready	38
One Day	39
Last Day	40
Moving	41
Pillow	42
Soon	43
Not Your Time	44
What You are Missing?	45
Dragonfly	46
The Last Good-bye	47
Rain	48
Maybe Somehow	49
Passing Seasons	50
New Day	51
Essence	52
Thanksgiving	53
The Journey I am now on	54
Signs	55
What Changed?	56
Patterns	57
Garage Sale	58
Giving Up	59
The Mall	60
Forgiveness	61
Your Other Side	62
Blue Angel	63
Our Love	64
Reflection	65
I'm Okay	66

Beautiful Man	67
Soft Wind	68
Home	69
Your Illness	70
I Still Weep	71
Forever	72
Remembrance	73
Happy Halloween	74
Path	75
New Tracks	76
Feelings	77
Afterword	78
About the Author	80
Resources	81
Author's Notes	83
Epilogue – Naj Wikoff	84

Acknowledgements

Looking back over the past five years since the death of my husband, Dennis Ryan, I realize that it has taken far more than the kindness and guidance of my friends and long walks on the mountain trails here in the Adirondacks to see me through this most difficult time of my life. Exceptional people, who were moved to reach out to pull me from one of the saddest places I have ever known, have played an essential role in my healing. Please know that I am forever grateful to each and every one of you for having touched me so deeply along my way.

I like to think that Dennis' many kind deeds throughout his life made a difference. Perhaps people were inspired to stay in touch with me and lift me up in part in memory of all his efforts to do just that while he was alive. He always encouraged others.

I would like to give special credit to a few exceptional people. Certain members of my family, certain friends, went above and beyond anything I might have expected and have remained by my side. Please know you are forever in my heart.

My sister Judy Scammell and her husband, Don, were with me throughout many a painful day and remain so even now. Barely weeks into his retirement, Don went back to what amounted to a full-time job helping me with the weighty matters to attend to after someone passes: bills, lawyers, selling the house, and so much more. I am forever grateful to you for standing by me, driving back and forth between Albany and Lake Placid weekly as you did. You spent hours listening to me in pain, seeing me through the aftermath of a tragic death.

My sister Mary Farr and her husband Dan, who live in Pennsylvania, were present in person whenever they could and always a phone call away with their love and support. For having worked together for years, Dennis and Dan had been like brothers.

I credit my sisters Judy and Mary for inspiring me to express my journey through poetry. They knew that writing was my way of dealing with life's hardships. Every time they saw me, they handed me another blank journal book. They spent hours listening to me read to them when I was still barely able to contain my emotions. My sister Mary became my editor. Her assistance and organizational skills have been invaluable for compiling this book. Without her dedication to this project, it would have been impossible for me to create what you now have in hand, a book born of my inspiration to help others, the thought that others may be helped by it, be it in some small way.

Mary's daughter Stanzi McGlynn had just returned from Peace Corps service in Africa when my husband died by suicide. She put her own life on hold and stayed with me day in and day out for two months. She helped me sort through many boxes of memorabilia. Thank you, Stanzi and Stephanie Farr, for your joyful remembrances of Dennis' life at his Life Celebration. Dennis adored you both.

Many other members of my immediate family have been supportive and loving throughout this challenge: Jay and Gun Rand, Janne Rand, Denja and Andrew Weibrecht, Ingrid Rand and her children Tanner, Tess, Anders and Tristin Stanton, Steve Rand, John and Terry Hathaway Rand, Tyler Rand and Owen Rand. I extend thanks to Dennis' brother Joe, his wife, Daisy, and their family members who were exceptional in their love and support. Nikki Righter Todd and her husband Jeb were very supportive, and Nikki's letters, books, and overall understanding of suicide helped me heal in more ways than I can express.

Dennis loved all his friends as brothers. Mario Pecoraro was such a friend and became a powerhouse helping me organize matters following Dennis' tragic death – another guardian angel flying to my side, and his wife JoJo who organized a two-day garage sale. Dale Davis, a great friend of Dennis and mine, was there for me since day one providing so much love and support.

Tevor Hough was like a son and brother to Dennis. Dennis was so proud of him and his accomplishments at Norwich University and beyond. I thank him for his heartfelt words in the **Forward** -- they mean the world to me.

Greg O'Brien has been the singing angel whose beautiful voice lifted us all up at Dennis' funeral. Sue Cameron put together the pictures and music for the gathering at which we celebrated Dennis' life. It made such a difference to see Dennis up on the screen big as life again. The kindness and concern for preserving the memory of Dennis shown by the Norwich Community of brothers has been so appreciated. A big thanks goes to John Harrity and Dave Whaley. Dennis loved you all.

My dear friend Denise Bujold gave of her love and guidance to keep me moving forward. She and her sister, Marcy Quinn, comforted me in the hours after I received the tragic news. They generously provided love, support, and food for so many. I thank Dr. Lewis Morrison and his staff, in particular, Lori Reisner whose warmth and big heart I will never forget. I learned the news while at work with them and they all helped me through those first moments.

Good friends Dan and Alice Crayon were present both before and after Dennis' death. Kindly they helped me with home duties, even mowing my lawn weekly until I moved. Joe Fiorile provided wonderful advice and knowledge. I could not have managed as well as I did without him. Debbie Cutler's kind legal expertise helped pave the way to my new life in more ways than one.

Ed and Lisa Weibrecht and their family deserve thanks for having helped me find a new home. Their care and generosity made such a difference, as did Peter Holderied and his family who helped me with the move.

Greg O'Brien and Patty Bona and many others helped organize my move back to Lake Placid. Donna and Bill Spellman, two of Dennis' oldest friends, were invaluable in moving me from Albany to Lake Placid in the pouring rain. Thanks as well to others who pitched in: Glen Stacey, Jim and Christine Meager, and Sue and Rich Frontera and the NPA Group for its assistance.

I thank Michael McGlynn and Ann O'Leary for offering me the job that kept my mind steady once I returned to Lake Placid. Thank you to Linda Wallace and Debbie Jarado of the organization Out of the Darkness for helping me get my feet back on the ground and helping so many others in dark places.

I thank the writers who read my poems and acknowledgements and shared their constructive advice: Caroline Welsh, Roger Mitchell, Renée Cosgrove, and Naj Wikoff. I am very grateful to Naj for seeing me through the publishing process and all who offered their expertise to help make my dream a reality. Bonnie Raymaley Kassen read my poems early on and encouraged me to publish this book of poems as she felt my journey would help others; I deeply appreciate her support and words of encouragement.

Now the real work begins, that of helping others by catching them before they go down a dark path. Today more than ever before, we know about suicide risk and assistance is available. Please pass this book on to people whom you either know or suspect to be in trouble, to their loved ones, to helping organizations, and to survivors in need of understanding and support. These poems are the record of my prayers along my trail. I now pray that my poems will encourage others in need of new directions to take the brighter path.

A special thanks to all my friends who helped me in so many ways. I love you all.

Forward

Trevor Hough

Lightning struck. In May of 2012, I was about to board a flight from Reagan National Airport when I checked my email as I habitually do and, suddenly and uncontrollably, I became dizzy and nauseous. My legs buckling under me.

"Subject: 'Sad News' It seems that Dennis took his life last evening . . . He shot himself and left a note for Barbara. This tragedy comes as a total shock to everyone . . . ."

Dennis Ryan was the cause and inspiration for this excellent book of poems by his beloved widow, the lovely Barbara Ryan. Dennis played a huge role in the lives of everyone whom he knew and befriended. I simply would not be the person I am nor where I am in life without his having taken a chance on a teenage kid from Lake Placid, New York, so many years ago. Dennis invested his boundless energy in others and served as a role model in every community in which he lived. His 1976 *Norwich University War Whoop Yearbook* quote summed up his larger-than-life personality: "You Ain't Seen Nothing Yet!" Sadly, he never reached out for help at the end, and that despite having helped so many other people throughout his life.

Life throws figurative lightning bolts at all of us. These often come with the same suddenness and power as real lightning. Deaths, divorces, accidents, diseases—these are life's lightning bolts that forcefully bear down on the fullest of lives. Nothing prepares survivors of suicide for what they will experience after the loss of a loved one at his own hands. The mixture of anger, pain, and sadness that those left behind feel is an overwhelming emotional charge that never entirely goes away.

In my lifetime including over 24 years of service in the US Armed Forces, I've known over a dozen people, mostly active or veteran members of the military, who have tragically taken their own lives — part of an epidemic of suicide striking our military. Not once did I or anyone close to these people see these suicides coming in the hours, days, and weeks prior to them. Life's problems are never made easier by ending a life.

Barbara found a measure of relief for her grief and anger through composing these poems. In publishing them, she hopes to reach others in need. If you are reading this book and thinking of harming yourself, please seek help. Talk to the very loved ones whom you would devastate. Learn how much people care and what different people have to offer you. Take strength from the poems in this collection such as "Path" or "New Tracks." Your life matters.

Barbara's words will also help survivors know that they are not alone and that their emotions are a normal reaction to their experience. To survivors I say: take your time to process what has happened but, please, reach out to your loved ones and community to heal together.

A wooden plaque hung on the wall at Adirondack Radio where I and the other Adirondack Radio Good Guys worked for Dennis. At its top were two words, "Promise Yourself," and below that were a dozen or so promises suggested for readers to make to themselves. One promise was, "To be too large for worry, too noble for anger, too strong for fear, and too happy to permit the presence of trouble." But a promise was missing from that plaque and should have been included with the others: "Promise everyone in your life that you will seek help when things get tough and, reciprocally, will make yourself available to your loved ones who need you."

We all need to make more time to tell the people in our lives that we love them and let them know that we're there for them always. Only by all doing more can we make a collective difference in the fight against suicide. Despair is an illness. If you explain what is happening to several people, at least one of them will rush to your aid. The transition Dostoevsky highlights in his short story, *The Dream of a Ridiculous Man*, is always possible. Why? Because your life matters:

"Here, suddenly, while I was standing and coming to my senses – suddenly my revolver flashed before me, ready, loaded – but I instantly pushed it away from me! Oh, life, life now! I lifted up my arms and called out to the eternal truth; did not call out, but wept; rapture, boundless rapture, elevated my whole being."

Author's Note

"Be kind, for everyone you meet is fighting a hard battle you know nothing about."

– Ian Maclaren

My husband Dennis Ryan was bigger than life. Very much a people person, he always empathized with people who were going through hard times. He was kind, had lots of energy, and was known for being intense. With these qualities, he helped to move the world around him in positive ways and led the many projects he worked on to a speedy completion. Whether driving miles to the funeral of a good friend's parent or involving himself in community affairs, Dennis was always present for others.

After the shock of his death by suicide on May 21, 2012 -- a suicide no one saw coming -- I fell into deep sadness, then depression. Looking back, I don't know how I would have survived without the love and support of my family and friends. Mine was a very slow recovery amidst the chaos of financial matters, moving from the cozy house we had shared and the city we had both loved, and dealing with endless details alone.

My long-time love of writing poetry helped me to find a new way of living my life. It provided me with a means for dealing with my extreme loss when I was alone and distraught. The poems started to come to me soon after the suicide and continue to do so often. I don't think this will ever cease. Eventually, I began to think that perhaps I too could find a way to help others, with my poetry.

The aftermath of a suicide is a long dark tunnel to walk through for those left behind. Extreme effort is required to get through each day, especially at the beginning. I have learned that the stages of grief that psychology and self-help books outline are unpredictable and ever-present in my life. There is no exact science of the grieving and healing processes. It is easy to slip back into the sadness of loss, especially at anniversaries and holidays. Each person grieves in their own special way.

I have been so fortunate to have the ongoing support of my family and friends. My wish is that, in some small way, my poetry will touch others in situations similar to mine. I want others to realize that it is possible to make it from the darkness of despair back into the light of hope.

My book of poems is also a call to those dealing with suicidal thoughts in their daily lives. Death by suicide is not the answer. Reading the thoughts of someone left behind may make it possible for you to grasp that there can be another way. Talk to someone. If that doesn't work, talk to someone else. Because your life matters and there is help for you out here.

In the back of this book you will find a list of organizations offering assistance to those in need of help. So many who ask for help are later glad they did and glad to be alive. My plea to you is: Never give up.

You chose to die so suddenly.
Why?

Eleven Weeks

It has been eleven weeks,
and my heart and head still do not meet.
I can no longer believe this is all a bad dream,
because when I wake up,
I can hear myself scream.
It has been eleven weeks of pure hell,
remembering the day
you shot yourself.
And when the news was delivered to me,
my knees gave way
and I fell to the ground.
I think there must have been angels all around.

What happened to believing?
Life has its up and downs
but you somehow forgot
that life is about cycles.

Too Late?

Was it too late to have one more date?
Why did you leave in such a hurry?
Why were you filled with such determination?
One more kiss on your lips,
and maybe I could have talked you out of this.
Why didn't you give me a chance to hear your plea?
Was it easier to end it all so suddenly,
pull the trigger,
and fall away from life?
And now I must stay here
without you near,
and live this tear-filled reality.
There is no escape for me,
my dear.

I will love you forever and ever,
but it will hurt.

Final Moment

You decided to end your life.
Now we are far away from our love.
I cry so often.
Why did you choose death
and not our beautiful life together?
In your final moment,
did you think of your wife?
Couldn't you imagine the pain
that would soon appear in her eyes?
In your final moment,
when you could not stop,
what was your final thought?
There must have been so much pain,
perhaps you were momentarily insane?
How did you hide it all inside?
I miss you so much,
a part of me feels I too have died.

3

When will it end? When will I mend?
When will the moon become whole again?
Will it help to patch my heart and soul when it does?

You

You are up there somewhere,
I am down here.
I do hope you are with the angels,
but I am wounded.
I am exhausted,
dealing with the details,
and mess of death;
and your tragic suicide.
I am a trembling sight.
My sleep brings on such frightening dreams;
nothing looks good right now.
You walked away from life and I ask you,
was that right?
You who loved the world so much.
You who I can no longer touch.
Though sometimes I can feel you in the room…
which helps a little…to ease my pain,
my oppressive gloom.
As I reach out to touch you,
I feel you go…and once again I'm alone
in the darkest place I've ever known.

You were a gentle soul with a big heart.

Nighttime

I reach out for you across the bed,
then I remember the man I love is no longer here.
I no longer can kiss your face
as I stare out at only empty space.
My tears roll over to your side,
never drying because you have died.
With all you and I had together,
do you feel that you are now better?
Do you sometimes visit me at night,
look at me…and know that this is not right?
Are you able to hold my hand,
and feel all the love I still have for my man?
I will weep forever for what you have willfully severed.
Please watch over me and help me to understand
why the love of my life
found it necessary to take his leave,
in such a way.
It is still so hard to believe.

I am in a dark place.
I can't remember your face.

No Final Good-bye

You left in such a hurry
no final good-bye.
Your kiss still remained on my lips
from the night before
that final trip.
I look for the answers
and I find none.
Were you so tired?
A burned out fire?
Was your heart scorched
from carrying around red hot coals?
What about all those cards you wrote to me,
filled with love and so many roses?
Did your death become just another goal?
You who were so good at reaching them.
Your pain must have grown too volatile and intense
for you to give up and go in such a way.
You who loved and lived life to the fullest.
Did you think my life would just go on?
How wrong you were.
If you only knew the pain you left behind.
It would have been easier for me,
to just go blind.

There are no answers...only sadness and grief.
Who were you? Who did you become?
How did you get that way? Who knew?
Regardless, no one could have gone
into your troubled mind without you first
giving them a key.

Is Death a Better Place for You?

Can you see the way you used to see?
Is this the way you wanted it to be?
You are buried in the ground.
Can you still hear all the earthly sounds?
Your handsome face was destroyed.
What a waste!
Your beautiful hair,
is it still there?
You must miss life... I can only guess.
Are you watching me as I go on?
Wishing you were still here...
and perhaps if you had stepped back a second
and really looked,
you would have seen
that you still belonged to life.

For a while we were two hearts that became one.

Life or Death

You left life for death.
Death not life,
was that right?
Only blackness and bleakness
you would meet.
You took a gun and the gun won.
Did your past and the happy times
all come back
right before you died?
In a flash,
you were gone.
Is death still where you belong?

Your fateful decision to leave left us
speechless and heartbroken.

Dreams

You came back in my dream
no longer human
your face distorted and pale.
You looked at me,
and stared an empty stare.
Have you forgotten my name
when you lost your own?
How sad that all we had is gone.
It took but a moment to make it all go wrong.
I will dream about you again,
dreams that never end.
But today it is hard to see you...
in a morbid state.

You blew your life away with a shotgun that day.
Everything seems frozen in time,
because you were still mine.
Never again will you feel the cold snow
because the blood in your veins no longer flows.

When

I have never felt pain like this before.
It hurts me to the core.
All my organs are under attack,
I am hurting so much,
because you won't ever come back.
My heart is an empty shell
that just wants to collapse.
My lungs can't catch a breath…
because of your death.
I shake inside,
thinking about the violent way you died.
You made us all believe that you were so strong.
When and where did it go so wrong?

Everything changes
nothing stands still.
Even a great fire must cool;
bad days always pass.

Torch

Are you now a volunteer
running a new show somewhere?
Are you missing all we had?
Are you sad?
Is there a torch up there?
An open flame always lit?
But the torch down here is gone.
The torch was your tremendous life.
How could you leave it?
How could you leave your wife?

Your past is all behind you now,
but know you are loved
for all time.

My Hero Soldier

I'm devastated
that you vanished so suddenly
to another dimension
where life is not our life.
How could you cross over in such a violent way?
You were like my hero soldier.
You died alone,
in a storm of emotion.
I forgive you.
I don't understand though.
How long did you plan this destructive end?
You were such a great man.
I wish we could speak together,
and I would ask you how it all came to be,
why did you let your guard down,
and how did you grow so desperate?

I hope you rest in such grace
because I know you
must miss this place.

Blown Away

You blew yourself away
on a day in May
all by yourself in a lonely place.
You took your life and destroyed your face,
seeming so ready to die.
You left a few letters and said good-bye.
All your family and friends were stunned.
This was a man who always won!
A hero,
a friend,
and my greatest love.
Did you not know how much you were loved?
We will never know why you died?
Why did you keep it all inside?

The sky has lost its stars now
since you took your final bow.
The moon is no longer
whole and my heart has grown cold.
You had no right to take its warmth away!

Cry

I didn't cry today.
I am getting stronger.
I may cry tomorrow
because I will never
get over this sorrow.
I didn't cry today.
I am getting stronger.
but I may cry next week
talking about you when I speak.
I didn't cry today.
I am getting stronger.
I may cry tonight
when I lie on our bed
with you nowhere in sight.
I will probably cry the rest of my life.
Never having my husband say
that he loves his beautiful wife.
The Lovely Barbara
no more.
It will never be like it was before.

Maybe one day we will sit on the moon
and our hearts will find a new tune.

Remember

Remember me if you can.
Can you come back again?
I would love to see your spirit
float around the room.
If anyone can make it back,
it would be you.
Can you stay a while with me,
explain to me why this had to be?
If you still have eyes
please look into mine and
tell me why.
What was so bad that you had to leave?
What happened to your belief in life…
no matter how hard
dealing with whatever was in the cards?
Now your choice is no longer yours
forced forever into eternity.
I miss you, my love.

There are no answers,
only more questions.

Alone

I came home to an empty house
and threw myself on our vacant couch,
I peered into your office room,
and felt such a sense of gloom.
You are no longer there,
and I am now alone.
My life has changed.
I cannot sleep.
My days lack joy.
It is hard to cook for one.
When it was always for two,
me and my Irish boy.

I am getting good at masking my pain,
but there is so much sadness that remains.
No one can really know how I feel.

Relief

Can you give me some relief?
Can you give me back some belief
in this life?
I believe I will hold you again someday,
perhaps in a different way,
yet death cannot be the end.
If I could ask one question it would be…
tell me why it had to end
this way?
The last morning we said good-bye,
had you already made up your mind to die?

Where do spirits go upon death?
Is it really better than being here?
Or do you beg for rebirth?

Tired

When did you get so tired,
you could not sleep?
Why didn't you speak?
Tell me all your thoughts,
I guess you forgot.
Whatever it was,
we could have worked through it,
with love and faith,
all things are possible.
I feel so lost.
so alone.
I wish you could please
come home.

Never again will you destroy my life.
Never again will I live in such sorrow.
Never again because hearts do
eventually mend.

The Beast

When you died,
I felt you lied.
We talked about living
into our old age together.
Surely we would make it to that stage.
Holding hands forever,
but now our story is
destroyed.
Are you happy where you are?
Have you become one of the stars?
Are you safe and free of pain?
Do thoughts of me remain?
Rest in peace dear husband,
now far away from the torment of your life,
have you finally killed
your haunting beast?

You were sure something great to me!
When did you begin to think
you were no longer a good enough man?

Wishing

I feel so alone in our bed.
I can no longer reach for your hand,
you no longer exist as a man.
I feel your spirit,
but not you.
How is it our life is through?
I miss all that we shared.
Didn't you know how much I cared?
I loved you every day of every year,
for every moment,
can you hear my plea?
Are you so much better off now,
instead of resting your head
next to mine?
Can you still think about our life,
do you ever wish you had me
once again?

You've gone away forever
without leaving me even one last love letter.

Painful Place

How did you hide it all?
I remember the times you said,
only a weak man falls.
When did you decide to let go,
and end up six feet below?
I wish I could have seen this hurting
human face to face.
You always were so convincing
as a man of strength.
You left so many hurt souls behind.
Do you know how much I miss our walks,
our meetings on the trail?
This all-encompassing sadness
is such a painful, bleak place to be.

Never again will we drink a glass of wine together.
Never again will you be mine.

Time

Does time bring healing,
and eventually a better feeling?
How long does it take?
Oh please say soon,
for my sake.
Each day that passes,
my heart aches…
As I think how much I miss my mate.
If you can still see me here,
in this weakened state,
Oh please,
help release me soon from my fear.
Soothe my soul,
and get me out of this black hole.
I do not know how to escape this place.

You became a falling star who felt
he no longer had a place to call home
you must have felt so alone.

Fate

Why did you give up your breath,
and Let in death?
Why did you decide your own fate?
Who gave you this power
to end your life once covered in flowers?
It was not your time,
you were still mine.
Why did you change your plan,
become a spirit not a man?

I tell you I miss you,
but no reply comes through.
You are now invisible
just like the air.

Who

Who will save me,
now that you are gone?
Who will love me?
Who will warm me when I'm cold?
I will no longer be yours to hold.
I can only envision you here,
and live with my own sweet and sour tears.
You must feel how much you are missed.
Is your new existence
all that you truly wished?
I hope you are safe from your pain,
and in your heart,
I still remain.
Sleep well D.R.
no matter how far away you are.

We followed our path,
but our path only took us so far.
Now we are forever apart.

Bad Dream

Has it hit you yet,
about your death?
Is there any sorrow
because you will have
no tomorrow?
When your eyes open,
you will be hoping
that this is only a bad dream,
and you are still among the humans.
Will you remember my face
and feel any disgrace?
Why did you lose your hope,
that all could improve,
and you would learn to cope,
because it all would eventually…get better.
It always does.
Oh how sad that
you left us all to wonder.
Now we will never really know,
what it was that put you under.

Now I speak to you at the grave,
asking you to help me to be brave.

One More Time

What happened to your mind?

You gave us no signs.

Where was the sadness in your eyes?

Did they show so much sorrow you would die?

I saw nothing,

a miss.

Not even that anything was different

in that last kiss.

When they first told me you died,

I thought it was a lie.

How could my lover, my hero, my friend

die like this in the end?

I want you back right now,

even if it means

you will take your final bow

one more time.

One more time,

please be mine.

You would hold my hand
always saying to me, yes you can!

Do You Still Sparkle?

Do you have bills to pay or work in heaven?
Or is it every day sleep until eleven?
Do you cry?
Can you fly?
Do you have feelings?
Is your life appealing?
Do you drink a glass of wine?
You must have so much time?
No worries,
since you have gone,
but how you got there was so wrong.
Do you wonder how I may be?
It should be you and I,
not just me.
If you can cry,
please cry me an ocean
so I may swim again,
and release me from this awful pain.
I will someday find you wherever you are,
and my eyes will sparkle like the stars.

Six Weeks

Six weeks since we spoke,
no hope?
A quick kiss,
and what did I miss?
A man bent on leaving,
giving up hope,
and not believing.
When did you lose control?
What made you choose your final role?
You who loved life,
and loved your wife.
Was it all lies?
Were you wearing a disguise?
Nothing could be so bad as death
causing eternal pain when you left.
Six weeks and I am still weak
from sorrow that will still come tomorrow.
I see no end to this pain,
and you are not here to blame.
I may never know why you left,
but in the deepest regions of my heart,
I will always grieve your death.

There are so many questions
I want to ask you and one of them is
who was this man I thought I knew?

Dark

I can't sleep,
my body is weak.
You have caused me so much pain,
tears fall like the pouring rain.
I toss and turn,
my heart burns.
I shout at you in the dark.
Are you still listening?
Do you feel the sparks?
You could have lived.
So many would give to have a life like yours.
You turned your back,
and your demons attacked.
How can you walk in heaven,
while I lie wide awake past eleven.
How do you sleep,
as I weaken?

When you went over the rainbow
where did you go?
Was it as beautiful as you thought it would be?
Have you gotten all that you wanted?

Fourth of July

You are missing the Fourth of July
because you chose to die.
Fireworks go on without you.
I can't believe this is true.
Your voice is missed,
so is your kiss.
I will try not to cry
on the Fourth of July.
In honor of you,
I'll wait until it grows dark and late,
and I am back home
where you and I can be alone.
Alone again another night,
just me and my shadow.
I only hope you are there to know how much
I really cared for and loved you,
always…. you will be my baby!

So much sadness has been spoken,
my tears may be less,
but inside it is all still a big mess.

The Truth About Life

You had so much fire within.
Too bad that only pain and destruction remain.
You had so much to live for.
In life,
you soared every minute.
When did the world get so confusing?
When did you choose not to remain?
Sometimes I feel I was partly to blame.
I didn't recognize you were so lost.
You had enough.
It had gotten too tough for you.
and you lost yourself and the realization
that things do eventually
get better.

I am in such despair.
I don't know if I will ever repair.
My heart has crumbled.
I feel lost in a dark tunnel.

Come Back

Can you come back to me?
I am in pain.
Can you see me?
I walk in the woods that we loved.
I am below,
you are above.
I sit on our bench and cry.
Why did you have to die?
You had years to go,
I loved you so.
Can you hear me scream?
We were always a team.
What happened?
You gave me no signs.
Come back and explain
why you gave up.

I am writing a letter
That you will never receive.
But right now,
I need to believe
you will hear me.

Are You Okay?

Are you okay today?
Are you happy and at peace,
now that your life has ceased?
Are you okay since that May day
when you decided not to stay?
Do you miss me just a little?
I miss you a lot.
Will you be watching as my life goes on?
Did you expect me to be so strong?
Are you okay today?
You and I no longer lie next to each other
when you left we were severed.
I am not okay!

I miss you so much.
I miss our talks and hearing your thoughts.
You left me in a terrible place.

July Third

July third and your voice will not be heard.
On the Fourth, not a single word.
It's a silence,
caused by violence.
Who gave you the right,
to take your life?
Why could you not spare me this pain,
and decide you should remain?
You are never coming back to me,
and my life is now under attack.
I am feeling I am at war with myself,
wishing I knew how much you needed help.
As always, I would have been there in every way,
if only you had stayed.

There is a storm,
and it's not leaving.
There is a hole in my heart
and I am still bleeding.

Goodbye

Goodbye is so bitter sweet.
Never really knowing for sure
if ever again we shall meet.
You took my dreams away
on that sunny day.
And left me all alone.
Did you cry just a little,
or were you frozen with fear?
When you pulled out that gun,
the demons won.
Did you have second thoughts,
but decided you were lost?
Oh how I wish I could have saved you,
and we would still be an amazing couple.

When the wind blows,
memories of us just seem to flow
through my mind and I go back
to so many wonderful times we shared.

Widow

I am a widow now.
We had many good years left.
It was always you and I,
and then you died.
I must go on and stay strong.
Some days are better than others
and sometimes I see other lovers,
and I miss our life,
as husband and wife.
I wish I could remember,
was there a clue?
Could you have survived?
But you surrendered your soul.
Oh my love,
I'll never know
why you chose to go?

If Only

If only I had not worked that day
maybe you could have stayed?
If only I had called your cell,
your voice might tell.
Tell me something was not right.
I could have helped you win the fight.
If only I had held you longer,
maybe you would have been stronger?
If only you had opened up more to me,
Your beautiful face I would see.
Instead I live a recurring dream,
dreams of losing you again and again.
If only you were still here,
the night would not frighten me so.
If only you were here with me,
instead of letting us go.

As I Get Ready

As I get ready to leave our home,
my heart aches
I feel so alone.
People come to buy our things,
more and more sadness does this bring.
All our years together,
more years could have made it better.
I can't bear to wash your robe,
all I want to do is smell your scent and hold it near.
As I get ready to move alone,
I can hear my heart moan.
As I get ready for a different life,
I will always be your wife.
As I get ready to leave,
it will still always be,
only you and me.

One Day

One day I will find you
sitting on the moon and waiting too.
Waiting for me to reach you,
hold you, and love you like we once did.
One day I will find you on a star.
I will stare into your eyes,
and ask you why?
I will forgive you for what you did.
One day I promise,
I will hold you again.
But only when God decides
when my life is to end.
Until then my love,
protect me if you are able.

Last Day

On the last day of your life,
you told me over and over
how much you loved your wife.
On the last day of your life,
was your plan already in sight?
Did you plan it for a year?
Did this plan ever fill you with fear?
You were always so strong,
but now I know that is not true.
When you dressed on that last day,
had your plan always been for May?
May brings spring and new life all around,
while yours was fading, waning and slowing down.
Tell me please,
on that last day,
what would have
made you stay?

Moving

I am moving from our home.
and I am all alone.
We have always moved together,
you and I were like glue and feathers.
It will be such a sad day,
when I look back and know I cannot stay.
A few more weeks before I go,
it hurts me so.
"This will be our home until we are
seventy-five," you said.
Oh how you lied!
How long had you been planning this awful act?
Soon I will be moving on to another place,
with so many beautiful memories
now tucked into my very worn suitcase.

Pillow

I hug your pillow and no longer you.
You made it permanent that you were through.
I saw nothing in your eyes,
that would give me a hint,
that you were planning to die.
You said you loved me,
so why?
I hug your pillow and not you,
I am so blue.
I wish I could ask you why you chose to die.
Life is so much better than death
you who so loved the beauty in life
and every breath.
I miss you every day and night,
and forever I will ask myself
why? Why did you not
reach out, ask for help,
and choose to win the fight?

Soon

Soon I will be gone to another place,
and all the memories will come along
because they cannot be erased.
They were all great,
until now.
Why you took your life and how?
I feel I should have seen a sign,
that you were far from fine.
Nothing seems to matter anymore.
I want my life back like before.
I wish you could have left me
a letter explaining
exactly why you wanted to die.

Not Your Time

You blew your face apart,
and my heart.
Did you shed a tear for me,
or was death all you could see?
No way out you said,
so now you are dead.
You will never come back
and I feel I have been brutally attacked.
Where was your strength
to fight for your life?
It was not your time,
or was it in your mind?
Where did you go that day,
when you decided you could not stay?
I feel I have been cheated of years,
there should have been more time for our love.

What you are Missing?

What you are missing?
Is our great time together,
and the kissing.
The chance to turn another age,
add another story to our page.
Getting together with our dear friends,
has come to a sad and tragic end.
What you are missing
is summertime fun,
walking near the camp in the woods.
But most of all,
you are missing me.
I am missing you.
You threw it all away,
now I am alone,
just one,
no longer a part
of being two.

Dragonfly

You have become my dragonfly.
You have died, but you are still alive.
You still dance in my heart,
even though we are apart.
You flutter all around,
and I feel somehow you have
found me again.
You stay for a while,
and my excitement is that of a child.
I stay very still hoping you will stay a bit longer,
you seem to know how much I miss you.
You loved the lake,
somehow you realize your big mistake.
You must miss your Caddy and me,
oh my dragonfly how can this really be?

You always said, don't look back.

The Last Goodbye

I will get ready to say goodbye
to a wonderful guy one last time.
Goodbye to our life in this home,
where now I feel so alone.
I will walk the grounds and pray
that peace will be found
for both of us somehow.
The last goodbye will be bitter sweet
until again we do meet.
I will look back one more time and know
even in this leaving,
you are still mine.
But as I leave on that day,
I will always wonder why,
why did it happen this way?

Rain

The rain is coming down hard.
Our separation is getting a bath
and I am remembering
your bold and beautiful laugh.
How you loved to walk in rain.
Did it help your pain or just give you time alone?
When the sun finally peeked through the clouds
and the light grew brighter,
were you in a happier place?
Or were the dark clouds always there
to attack you anytime, anywhere?
Did the rain ever really give you solace?
Did the sun ever make you think
you had finally won?

I must move.
The house is almost bare and empty.
All our dreams will stay behind,
But you will come along with me
In my heart and mind.

Maybe Somehow

Every day I wake up alone.
I wonder do you miss our home?
Are you okay in your world beyond?
Nothing here is right any longer.
You left me on a beautiful sunny day,
behind a dirty dumpster your lifeless body lay.
I will always wonder,
if only I had not gone to work,
maybe somehow I could have convinced you to stay.

Life is a hard rough road to travel,
but life is worth so much more than gold.

Passing Seasons

Snow is falling and it is now the season that
we once celebrated with great joy.
Seasons have died and so have you.
And for what reason?
Seasons come and go,
I still miss you so.
Your pain was hidden in the grasses of spring,
now turned to dust
in the leaves
that autumn brings.

Day by day, living is where I want to stay.
Day by day, I become stronger,
and I am no longer afraid.

New Day

Day by day a spark begins to grow within,
it starts to fill this emptiness,
it ignites a flame,
and I begin to embrace life again
and all that remains.

It is too late for you to join life again,
but perhaps there will be more
awareness to help others,
whose pain we may yet discover.

Essence

It has now been six months
since I lost you all at once.
Do you know what you left behind?
What you brazenly took from me,
was no less than the essence of my life,
and all that it defined.
How dare you leave me this way.
Could you not muster the courage
to reason it out,
to stay in spite of doubt?

In suicide no one wins.

Thanksgiving

It is now Thanksgiving and I am barely living.
You are no longer here to cherish,
I only have memories
and thoughts of you and of our past.
Suicide does not win anything.
You are missing abundant years,
and I am shedding a river of tears.
I thank God for all the time I had with you.
Wherever you have gone are you missing me too?

The Journey I am now on

The journey I am now on is to free
your spirit from my heart.
I must let this sorrow end.
I must allow my heart to mend.
I must survive your suicide.

*Sometimes I reflect
on our life and
I feel so lucky to
have been your wife.*

Signs

They all ask me,
were there any signs?
I try to remember back
to different situations and times.
You had your moods,
you always did,
but nothing appeared so bad to me.
You were intense.
You'd always say…
anything that was a problem
it will all work out soon,
and you were off again.
You were always helping everyone else.
You must have become so tired and spent.
You gave and gave,
if you can call that a fault?
You never knew when to rest.
You left so prematurely,
when you seemed at your very best.
They all ask me…Were there any signs?
I say no, only that he told me
he loved me all the time.

I must accept that you are gone.
And honor you by living my life through,
finding some source of joy once more.

What Changed?

I feel like hell,
I am alone with no one to tell.
You were my lover, my best friend,
and then you made it all end.
Such a tragedy!
You'd always say
that giving up was never
an option in your life.
So, what changed?
Why did you leave me behind,
this time?
We'd been through so many ups and downs,
we endured them all together.
Surely, you must have known that
material things come and go.
We never needed to eat on golden platters.
We weren't like that.
You were all that ever mattered.
What changed,
for you?

You were a man of more self-worth
than I had ever known.
So when and why
did you start feeling so alone?
So distraught? So tormented?

Patterns

I feel as though I did not do enough
to save you.
I should have realized more,
You suffered in silence.
It must have drained you to the core.
I regret not understanding
how your life had become
so difficult and so demanding.
I clearly was not conscious
of your torment.
I was so used to your humor
to your positive attitude,
tremendous strength
and great fortitude.
I often forgot how sensitive you were.
Forgive me.
Now everything hurts inside,
and my heart is no longer in my chest,
It lies buried with you
deep within the earth.

Your shoes and suits
go home with someone else
and my heart just melts.

Garage Sale

Your friends helped me
sell your personal things
and our history,
making it easier for your wife.
As I go through the pictures and possessions,
remembering all our precious times
filled with hope and laughter,
I am once again in shock
that you are gone forever,
and no longer mine.
Your choice to make life end,
made you miss a great time with friends.
The dreams of planes, and boats and cars
along with me,
were traded so ruthlessly.
You enjoyed a good garage sale,
but you are no longer here to enjoy
no more drives in Caddy, no more goals to reach.
The end of our lives together.
So what will tomorrow bring?

Giving Up

You missed another dinner.
I drank a glass of wine,
it was your favorite kind.
Every day friends stop by and say
how much they miss you,
and I say me too,
your death has made me forever blue.
I go to work,
I drink coffee,
I go home,
to what is now like a twilight zone.
I live my days and nights
trying to imagine just what you were fighting?
How did your life-long beliefs
that I shared and witnessed
for twenty-five years,
evaporate so quickly?
You'd say so often,
it rings in my ears,
work hard, accept failure, move on and your goals
eventually will be reached.
The very thought of these words
brings me to tears.

On that sunny day,
there were no visible stars
to guide you out of your darkness.

The Mall

I cried walking in the mall today.
It was our Sunday thing to do.
We'd walk hand in hand,
how I loved being with my man
we'd watch couples
who were like us.
Inspired by the joy of each other.
I am without you now,
wishing you were here.
I saw others notice my tears,
but no one really cares.
The Mall is full of strangers,
no friends anywhere.
I don't think I'll go back for a while,
there is nothing there to make me smile.
It only brings back memories of you.

It was a beautiful sunny day,
and you let nothing get in your way.

Forgiveness

The days move along,
and slowly,
I sense the brightness of life
move into my sorrow.
Now knowing each day
it will get a little better tomorrow.
I still hear your voice though,
but you made your choice.
I forgive you for leaving,
but I can't forget how you
no longer chose to believe
that life is better than death.
And it is the hardships,
as well as the successes,
that we must learn to accept.
I forgive you for not asking for help,
but I will never forget how you left.

I am a hurting soul,
 and my heart
is empty right now.
Listening to the radio,
I hear our songs,
and I am left speechless.

Your Other Side

Time is no longer on my side,
much of my heart has already died.
Time is the healer they say,
I wait for the healing each and every day.
Time is moving so fast,
but my pain seems to last and last.
A blue sky once made me smile,
and gave me such hope.
Today I am feeling only distress.
Once you made a plan with me,
to honor and to cherish forever,
until death do us part.
But you took it upon yourself,
to sever that sacred bond
in such a dark way.
You had another side that I never knew.

Sleep is my only release.
Sleep and dreams are where we still meet.

Blue Angel

Are you now a blue angel?
Filled only with regrets?
Are your wings pointed towards the earth
hoping you can start a new rebirth?
I know you have gone from this life,
but what you did was above and beyond
all that any human being
considers wrong.
You can't come home again,
only those who live
their lives can.

Sorrow today,
sorrow tomorrow,
sorrow is now
my constant companion.

Our Love

I climbed a mountain today,
and felt you in the clouds with me.
I felt the wind upon my face and
I felt our love was still in place.
I felt you deep within my soul,
and your love took hold.
You left me to carry on without you,
but you must carry on
without me too.
I'll climb more mountains through the years,
and I will cry more tears.
My life must go on however long.
I will miss you all the days of my life,
but I will always hold our memories within my heart.
You gave me so many good ones
for so many years.
Our love was better than any love song.

There was no one there,
but we all heard the doorbell ring
on the eve of your passing.
Was that you saying you are still alive
somewhere and that we do go on?

Reflection

There is a saying
when a person
may be thinking of giving up,
if they hold on a little longer,
everything changes,
and dreams survive.
It is true that you were tightly wired,
with an ego that could have
played a role in the unraveling
of what became your
tormented soul.
You had an inner world that drove you,
but its intensity was not always seen.
You were such a gentle man,
always helping others first
putting your needs last.
I know there is a lesson here somewhere.
To maintain balance in this life,
and give our surplus and that's all.
The doors are closed.
My whole body aches right down
to my toes.
I'll never get back
what I once had with you.

I guess you loved me,
but not enough to stay.

I'm Okay

It is three-months since that day.
I feel you must be in disbelief
all the pain and grief your death has caused.
I believe even in death
you must feel some regrets.
Your spirit must remain for a while
to try to claim your lost domain.
It must be so unreal
to know you can no longer
feel all the life you had.
Your spirit must be so lost.
You cannot come back at any cost.
I'm okay today,
but I know your spirit
can no longer stay.
You must find what you were seeking,
but it is life
that I am keeping.

Hello Baby!
I miss that!
I no longer hear this happy sound
now that you have passed
and are in the ground.

Beautiful Man

Beautiful man,
you have washed away
like ocean sand.
You have become part of the earth,
and left so much hurt.
You are like a river running away
never to return because
of that day.
Beautiful man,
you had a plan.
you decided that life
meant nothing anymore,
and left for the unknown
to explore.
The earth holds you now
in its grasp,
and I only have memories
of our past.
Beautiful man,
that was a terrible plan.

They say that time does heal,
but they are not the ones who feel
this tragedy as I do.

Soft Wind

There is a soft wind blowing
around and within.
I miss your great smile
and sparkling eyes….
it was all taken away when you died.
I miss everything we had.
I miss the good and the bad.

Go away... bad dreams!
Life is so much more than it seems.

Home

I am home,
and so are you.
In different homes,
but both alone.
My home is among the blue mountains
and green trees.
which you once knew,
and now can no longer see.
Yours is a place I have not been,
a place where I hope your
heart and soul will mend.
I someday hope to see your home,
but for now,
my love,
I will stay on earth
alone.

Time has taught me one thing,

that down deep you were   # Your Illness

a troubled human being.

You'd always go above and beyond

what was expected of any human being.

You were such a chameleon

blending into any setting

and still larger than life,

the brightest star

in the room.

We could never really see the man

behind the blazing light.

Even your closest buddies

never saw the inner chaos and confusion,

we came later to discover.

You'd take charge of all situations

like a combat soldier.

You were so driven,

and left even me,

unable to detect your lack of clarity.

Had you shared anything

of your torment and deep pain,

it might have helped you remain

and we would still have you

warming our hearts,

and our lives

with your humor, pranks and laughter.

Thinking back though,

sometimes you were intensely lost in thought,

staring into the woods you loved so much…

and somewhere along the line,

you got caught in a darkness, so unkind,

that would not let you pass unscathed.

They all look to me for the answer.
I have none.

I Still Weep

I still weep,
Weep for your life.
I loved you so much.
I was your wife.
The devastation you left in your path,
has left a terrible aftermath.
You have left me to explain why
you had died.
I can't explain!
I cry when I speak.
When I can get the words out,
I tell them my great love for you.
I tell them how sad I am that you wanted to leave,
that your illness took the best part
suffocating you and your heart.

You are part of my eyes,
I still see you.
You have not died.

Forever

Death is forever.
And our love you severed.
You told me you wanted me
to have a good life.
But you are no longer my husband,
and I am no longer your wife.

Eighteen years today
we were married.
You left me with many thoughts
but the last one I wish you had not.

Remembrance

What are you thinking?
I often would ask.
Perhaps you were thinking
that your earthly life would not last too long?
Sometimes you would look out into space
and a look of sadness
was sketched
upon your face.
During these times your eyes were drawn
and lacking any definite expression.
You always said everything was fine
and quickly changed the subject.
In hindsight, I think something in your heart
had gone missing.
Now I must try to live my life
and become
accustomed to your absence.
There are so many good memories,
they will help me carry on.
So, for now,
I will pack up my sorrows
and continue on my life's journey
without you.

You loved September.
but, of course, you no longer remember.
You have no mind or brain,
and nothing of your body remains.
I must now kneel at your grave
and pretend that I have gotten so brave.
I tell you I miss you,
but no reply comes through.

Happy Halloween

You are missing our beautiful pumpkins
and the dressed-up munchkins.
You loved Halloween,
with all the neon costumes and ghoulish masks.
You always said,
buy good treats,
later knowing, your mouth and they would meet.
A glass of wine in hand,
waiting for the doorbell to ring,
you seemed so happy with everything.
I will now sit alone
and wait for the little ones
to come to my new home.
I will put on a happy face
inwardly knowing
that I am alone.
Happy Halloween…my departed soul.

The moon is whole again.
My heart did not wither and die.
I know the storms are not that far away,
still the sun is out today
and beckoning me to feel
its warmth once more.

Path

I am on a different path now,
but following dreams I still have.
There is always a path that is dark at first,
but the more I walk it, the more I see a glimmer,
like specks of firelight in the distance,
they beckon me.
There have been roots that have tripped me.
and I have fallen hard,
but I always stand once more,
I never give up.
There are dark shadows that come and go,
but there is a brightness that always takes hold of me.
Yes, I am on the right path now.

New Tracks

Since you left,
I have changed.
I have lived and let go of a lot of pain.
My tracks have been left on many mountain tops,
firmly embedded in the deep white snow.
My heart is feeling more at peace.
I had to let you go with time,
but all the memories
are still mine.
Since you left,
I have grown.
and my new home
is surrounded by mountains
whose colors and beauty have
beckoned me back to life.
This is where
I now choose to roam,
and spend my days enjoying life
knowing with every fiber of my being,
that each day is a true blessing
to be honored and revered,
with not a second to waste.

Feelings

I know you continue to be present in my life.
I can still feel you in the wind,
the sun, and
even the slightest breeze,
somehow knowing we are still as one.
You will always live within me.
I will feel you in my heart beat,
and our souls do meet as I sleep.
At times, I feel you in my imaginary hold.
My senses open to a higher realm,
and I kiss your lips and feel your breath,
nothing can steal times we still share such as this,
even if they are merely imaginary,
not even death
can take away the magnificent colors
we once shared in life.

Afterword

Dennis Ryan was the love of my life. He was a gentle soul with a huge heart. Perhaps his heart was bigger than the average and that was why he gave so much to others.

He loved his family and me more than himself. He loved his friends, as they were his family too. His passions were many, but one of his primary passions was being involved in the lives of others. He was a good listener. When he talked with you, you felt special, as if you were the only person in the room. He was a small-town guy, but he drew in a city of friends.

The saying he was well known for was, "Failure is not an option." He was a Norwich University graduate, a disciplined person who had great respect for the Military life in general. His father was a Pearl Harbor survivor. My father was an 82nd Airborne soldier who survived all the major campaigns of World War II. It made sense that Dennis was deeply involved with the Veterans' causes throughout his life and right up until his death.

Dennis was always full of surprises. He especially loved the simple things in life. He was particularly passionate about music, and so he spent most of his professional life in the radio business. He started out as a disc jockey in college and, eventually, his experiences grew into management and ownership.

He loved movies and holding hands, chocolate and red wine, and especially our Christmas Eves together. He was a big fan of holidays in general and participated in the Fourth of July to the point of becoming a licensed pyrotechnic: he set off many fireworks over the years. He enjoyed flying and, as a licensed pilot, flew whenever he could. He worked with NASCAR for a time then Help Wanted.com, and finally became a financial business consultant.

A funny story about *my guy* to end on: one Thanksgiving, the restaurant we were at ran out of pumpkin pie -- my favorite. The next year, Dennis actually brought a pumpkin pie to the restaurant, which we had been frequenting for years, so that I would have my favorite pie for dessert, should they be momentarily out, and not be disappointed. He became the "pumpkin pie guy" at that restaurant forevermore!

He loved his 1976 Eldorado Cadillac so much. He called it *Big Red* and took such wonderful care of it, just like he did of me.

Our Sundays were mostly spent on taking road trips in *Big Red* with the top down, just cruising backcountry roads – always made *my guy* smile a lot.

He used to walk in our door bellowing, "Honey, I'm Home," imitating Jackie Gleason of the Honeymooners, one of his favorite shows growing up. He loved bells and even hung a big bell at work, ringing it each time he'd come in the door and saying there too, "Honey, I'm Home." Of course, the girls at the office all loved him too.

My guy will remain forever inside my heart.

"No one believes that death is the end.

If after a day's harvesting he sees the sheaves shine,

And the grain smile as it pours into his hand."

– Rene Char

About the Author

Barbara Rand Ryan lives in Lake Placid, New York, where most of her family resides. She likes to hike the mountain trails and believes that they have helped her heal and embrace life's joyful moments again. She is a yearly volunteer for the "Out of the Darkness" suicide-prevention events, an awareness organization that helps provide comfort and financial support to those in need.

In her youth, Barbara traveled the world on Norwegian freighter ships with her best friend Denise Wilson and lived in Norway for a time. Years later, she survived what might have been a tragic sailing accident in the Atlantic Ocean: a major storm capsized the small sailing vessel that she and the crew were planning to deliver to Saint Lucia in the Caribbean. Luckily, they were rescued by a South Korean freighter ship 800 miles east of Bermuda.

Her courage and energy have helped Barbara keep her spirits up. Barbara believes that it is the beautiful Adirondack setting that invigorates her and has helped her back onto the path to living a full life again.

She thanks Dennis for having encouraged her to return to school in Elmira, New York, where she enrolled in a dental assistant program. She worked in the dental field for over fifteen years. She also thanks Dennis for having inspired her to take a challenging Dale Carnegie course. Barbara feels that the course may have helped her develop the fortitude and stamina it has taken to reach out and share her heart-felt story through her poems. It is her greatest hope that this book will inspire others who are left behind to carry on and find the light again. It is also a plea for those with suicidal thoughts to seek the help that is available to them today.

"It's always too soon to quit." -Norman Vincent Peale

Resources

* A percentage of the proceeds from the sale of this book will be used to support agencies working to prevent suicide and as listed here as resources.

National Suicide Prevention Lifeline

1-800-273-8255

Or text Connect to 741-741 **(Crisis Text Line)**

Veterans Crisis Line

800-273-8255 then press 1 or Text 838255

www.veteranscrisisline.net

In Essex County, NY

Essex County Mental Health Services

Monday to Friday 8:00 AM – 5:00 PM 518-873-3670

Toll Free Emergency Services: 888-854-3773 (24-7)

Mental Health Association Hopeline: 800-440-8074 (24-7)

Essex County Suicide Prevention Coalition: 800-440-8075

www.facebook.com/essexcountysuicidepreventioncoalition/

The mission of the Essex County Suicide Prevention Coalition is to work together as a community to increase suicide awareness and prevention. Contact them for schedule of events, workshops, and or to request programming in your community or for your organization.\

Suicide Prevention Center of New York (State)

www.preventsuicideny.org

Suicide can be prevented. Help prevent suicide by knowing the facts, learning the warning signs, and where to get help. An excellent form of training is safeTALK, a half day of alertness taining available for people 15 or older. For information:

www.livingworks.net/programs/safetalk/

Essex County mental Health Services has staff training in safeTALK and can make such workshops available.

Events

Out of Darkness Walks

The American Foundation for Suicide Prevention is the leading national non-profit organization exclusively dedicated to understanding and preventing suicide through research, education, and, and advocacy. Out of Darkness Walks are their signature event and held in over 350 communities across 50 states. The Adirondack-North Country Walk is held annually around October first on the speedskaing oval in Lake Placid. For more information contact the Essex County Mental Health Services.

The American Foundation for Suicide Prevention:

www.afsp.donordrive.com

Books

On Grief & Grieving: Finding the Meaning of Grief Through the Five Stages of Loss

Elisabeth Kubler-Ross, M.D. and David Kessler

Healing After Loss: Daily Meditations for Working through Grief

Martha Whitemore Hickman

Author's Notes

Denial

Anger

Bargaining

Depression

Acceptance

All are evident in my poetry and never in any order. Like a flash they can appear, as grieving is an on-going and even a lifelong process.

EPILOGUE: For Barbara

Naj Wikoff

The arts are a great vehicle for sharing our stories, as Barbara does so well in this volume of poetry. The arts can help us connect with the experiences of others and give voice to emotions that would otherwise engulf our lives. The process of expressing feelings in words on a page, images on canvas, and emotions in dance, song, or music can help lessen our anxiety and enable us to take control and ownership of our lives. The outcome of our artistic expression can let others know that they are not alone, that someone else is living with challenges similar to theirs.

Even when confronted and expressed, pain is never completely erased; it can, however, be reduced. It can be set aside during the creative act in ways that reduce its power. Ultimately, pain becomes incorporated into our lives, like a scar from an old injury. It may ache from time to time but no longer owns us.

In my experience, combining involvement in the arts, getting out in nature, participation in complementary therapies such as Yoga, Reiki, and massage, and ongoing connections with people, friends, and family, is a recipe for bringing balance into one's life – all this coupled with helping others and a dash of humor.

Barbara has fully embraced a healing approach. She has gifted us with her vulnerability and authenticity illustrated in her poetic journey. I am humbled by her generosity and grateful for her willingness to be so open in sharing her experience with the public. I am thankful for a lifelong connection to her and to her family, a family that has always made a difference for others and cared deeply about community.

I encourage readers of these poems to create their own poems or lyrics, to put brush to canvas, pencil to paper, or let their bodies give movement to music. Whether you go public with what you create, share it with a friend, family member, or member of the helping professions is your choice.

The first step may be the hardest, but once made, the second and third will be easier. Barbara too started with just one word, then added a second. That's all it took. And we are grateful.

92201299R00057

Made in the USA
Columbia, SC
28 March 2018